The Sublime Boy

THE SUBLIME BOY

The Poems of
WALTER DeCASSERES

With An Introduction By
BENJAMIN DeCASSERES

ISBN13: 978-0-9885536-7-5

This edition prepared by Kevin I. Slaughter
for Underworld Amusements.
WWW.UnderworldAmusements.com

Further information available at:
WWW.BenjaminDeCasseres.com

FROM
THE ALMIGHTY PRESENCE
IN WHOSE DEPTHS
I ETERNALLY REPOSE
I DEDICATE MY POEMS DONE ON EARTH
—THROUGH THE MEDIUM OF MY BROTHER—
to
OUR BELOVED BIO

CONTENTS

Poetry is a bouquet laid on a Tomb.
— Charles Morice

WALTER DᴇCASSERES

I

WALTER DeCASSERES was born in Philadelphia on August 12, 1881, and threw himself into the Delaware River some time during the night of February 4, 1900. His mysterious disappearance caused a great deal of comment in the Philadelphia papers, on one of which, *The Press*, he was employed as a copyholder in the proof-room at the time of his death. His body was found on April 1 of the same year by some workmen doing river work at the foot of Arch Street. He was identified by a library card in his pocket. He was buried in Adath Jeshurun Cemetery, in Frankford, Philadelphia, on April 3.

These poems were written between his sixteenth year and the time of his death at eighteen years and nearly six months. I rescued them from among old school copybooks and some later notebooks. The poems were scribbled—sometimes in ink, sometimes in pencil—very carelessly on the first pieces of paper that came to hand—sugar bags, the back of bills and torn bits of white paper. I have held them for twenty-six years with only a vague thought of having them published "some day" because of their great and intimate value to me personally.

For when I read these poems the very fragrance and aroma—the distilled, unearthly essence—of the exquisite soul of Walter DeCasseres bathes me not only psychically but physically. He was literally a part of me, and in his poems I have always been able to summon the immaterial part of him to mingle with my own emotions and visions. So I resolved, many times, never to have his fragile creations published, but to let them die with me. But I have shown them to so many discriminating lovers of poetry (in whom the personal equation could not possibly enter) who have said such fine things about them that I have at last resolved to have them published.

II

I lived with Walter from the day of his birth until about three months before his suicide, for which I had been patiently and calmly waiting for more than two years, and which I looked upon, and still look upon, with the profoundest satisfaction. I slept with him for years, knew his every thought, his every mood—: and knew he had been planning suicide for two years—or, rather, profound fatalist that he was, watching for the summons to step out of this world.

From his fifteenth year onward the look on his face, asleep or awake, was, I'm lost—please show me the way back Home! He had a startled, ethereal expression; a breathless, hungry look. When he walked—quickly, nervously—he always gave me the impression of a boy hurrying into another dimension. His face was pale. The features were fine, exquisite. His eyes were brown. His small—almost tiny—mouth in the last year of his life had assumed a tense, bitter expression. He was slight, but always in perfect physical health. At a miscellaneous gathering—a funeral, I believe—at which Walter, in his seventeenth year, was present a woman asked her companion, pointing to Walter, "Who is that young man with the profile of a god?" He had a wide, high forehead, like the blank wall of a Greek temple.

III

Walter DeCasseres was a genius of the most angelic and devastating kind. Lucifer and Christ lived in the house of his soul. He was the most terrible nihilist and the most implacable no-sayer that it is possible to conceive. To him, there were no values—there could not possibly be any values—in a valueless and meaningless universe. At fifteen he was as completely disillusioned as Buddha, Omar and the author of "Ecclesiastes." God, Love, Art, Immortality—of what use were they? "Why?" "Well, and what then?" were the only replies he ever gave to those who tried to impress him with the idea that life was worth living just for the adventure.

He was born ill-at-ease, and he always showed it—from puberty (before puberty he was a normal, bright, play-loving boy, although as early as ten years of age there were heralds and presages in his face of the coming war with God and Man). He had an instantaneous vision shortly after puberty of the vanity of all things past, present and to come.

He had a vast pity for all created things. He often emptied his pockets of his spending money to the first beggar on the street. He could have killed with the same nonchalance—for, he asked, what difference does it make in eternity what you do? To obey his impulses was the only law he knew—and he obeyed them without regard to the suffering that it might bring on others. Let others do the same, was his answer.

Family ties were to Walter a superstition. Father, mother, home simply meant nothing to him. They were purely accidents. To soothe the agony of his spiritual life, he went on regular man-sized sprees from his sixteenth year. Alcohol threw him into another dimension, veiled reality and the horror of his shabby environment—hence, to him, it was good. He always acted like a being who lived absolutely beyond good and evil, although, of course, he had never heard of Nietzsche or Stirner. He was an Avatar of Negation.

IV

The suicide of Walter DeCasseres will naturally call to mind the death of Thomas Chatterton, the famous English boy poet who committed suicide by taking poison in his London lodgings in 1770. The two—Walter DeCasseres and Chatterton—were both precocious geniuses. Chatterton's suicide was caused by material need. Starvation stared him in the face and a little money could have saved him. His *Via Dolorosa* was financial. The *Via Dolorosa* of Walter DeCasseres was purely spiritual. He was a Boy of Sorrows. Nothing could have saved him. On the day his cradle was made Fate fashioned his Golgotha.

His suicide was philosophic. It parallels, among the ancients, Lucretius, who was self-slain, and among the moderns Otto Weininger, who took his life while still in his early twenties. Gerard de Nerval, that French poet and prose writer of exquisite sensibilities, hanged himself in an obscure street in Paris in 1855; but he was in his forty-sixth year, and his suicide was caused by his mode of life, which bore a striking resemblance to that of Francois Villon.

The philosophic suicide is the rarest and sublimest gesture that I know of. It is the final judgment of Intelligence before Life and its Author. It is a triumph over life and a triumph over death. Walter DeCasseres as a boy sat in the High Tribunal of his intelligence and tried the Author of his being. He found him guilty. As it was not in his power to sentence or exterminate Life, he removed himself, leaving to those who liked it to continue to dance to the Devil's Tarantelle played by the blind and deaf Beethoven of the Stars.

Walter was a vast reader of great authors from his fourteenth year onward. In the papers which I found after his death were pages of philosophic epigrams and pensees copied from the books that this wonder-boy was reading. The range, taste and depth of his intellectual life are revealed in the thoughts that he culled (written carefully in ink and with the name of the author and the book after each one) from Victor Hugo, Aristotle, Anaxagoras, Emerson, Diderot, Buckle, Bacon, Ella Wheeler Wilcox, Pythagoras, Montaigne, Carlyle, Seneca, Flammarion, Thomas a Kempis, Fontenelle, Helvetius, Plutarch, Tertullian, Horace, Lecky, Bossuet, Shakespeare, Kant, Lamartine, Alfred de Vigny, De Musset, Hood and Sainte-Beuve.

On another page he had put down one hundred and four

names of philosophers and historians—"works to be read for study of philosophy in historical order," he says at the top of the page. Among the names I find Plato, Origen, Plotinus, St. Augustine, Abelard, Duns Scotus, Jacob Boehme, Lewes, Fabre, Bruno, Hobbes, Descartes, Condillac, Hume, Hegel, Schopenhauer, Spencer, Comte, Montesquieu, Darwin, Ritter, Zeller and Fichte. How far he got with this titanic task I do not know.

I do not believe that any prose he ever read influenced him much. He seemed to know what all the thinkers were going to say after the first five pages, and the book generally went back to the library. He lived with and was influenced by the poets, I think—above all, by Poe, Keats, Blake and Shelley. He is close kin of Heinrich Heine, whom, I am certain, he never read.

He used to lie for hours on the couch with his eyes closed, absolutely moveless. A profound sigh would sometimes escape him. I knew he was not asleep—and knew where his soul was; and he knew that I knew.

Walter and I seldom spoke to one another. We communicated silently, understandingly, intuitionally—being twin souls.

BENJAMIN DeCASSERES
New York, August 12, 1926.

LIFE

We are but little children, after all,
And this great world of ours a darkened room,
With God a huge, fantastic shadow on the wall
That ever lures us into deeper gloom.

THE POET

The Poet's thought is like the sweetest rose
Plucked never by a mortal hand before,
That breathes a lovely fragrance where it grows,
And cannot die, but lives forever more.

The Poet's tone mayhap is one of gloom,
The sigh of God translated into words;
A Shakespeare's or a Byron's note of doom
Is sweeter far than morning chant of birds.

The Poet's life is as an endless dream;
He dwells far up in boundless realms of air,
And catches Heaven's sacred, mystic gleam—
He knows not how, nor why, nor where.

REMEMBRANCE

Sing me once more the songs of old
That I again may hear thy tone,
So like it seems an angel's own;
Ere death has come, ere life has flown,
Ere tongue is mute and lips are cold
Sing me once more the songs of old.

Sing me once more the songs of old
That echo through my heart and brain,
Through weary, weary years of pain—
Let me but hear them once again;
Ere tongue is mute and lips are cold
Sing me once more the songs of old.

Sing me once more the songs of old,
The sweet, sweet songs of long ago,
When hearts leaped high with love's bright glow,
The love that only youth can know.
Ere tongue is mute and lips are cold
Sing me once more the songs of old.

O love, mine eyes are filled with tears,
The night comes on, the weight of years—
Ere tongue is mute and lips are cold
Sing me once more the songs of old.

PHANTOMS

A group of phantoms in the Halls of Death
That hand in hand amid the wastes of night
In trembling terror stand with bated breath,
Each compassed by a pale, reflective light
That seems forever on the wane.
And some there are who murmur, "It is Fate,"
And some cry out in fear, while others wait
In faith and trust that God will lead aright,
But ever wait in vain.
For dimmer grow the lights as years pass on,
Until at last they fade and die away.
And why this happens none may say,
And none may know whereto his friend has gone.

THE ROSES

They laid her gently in the grave, with two roses on her
    breast,
A white rose and a red, and laid her hands at rest—
But from her breast I plucked the white and left the rose of
    red,
And the rose of white has faded not, though long has she
    been dead;
And through the night, when the moon is bright, down
to her grave I steal,
And on the sod, in the sight of God, down by her side I
    kneel,
And I pray for the day when by her side in the sleep of death
    I lie—
When fade those roses white and red I, too, shall surely die!

THE BATTLE OF THE PASSIONS

From out of the depths of the night,
A blood-red battalion they come,
They laugh, for with them lies the might,
And they know we shall have to succumb,

Heart-eating, venomous worms,
Brain-burning, horrible things,
That make the heart shudder and pale
And shatter the soul with their stings.

Silently onward they press,
And, writhing around and beneath,
They sting and they pierce with their fangs
And bite with their terrible teeth.

Soon—soon the dread battle is over,
But the conquerors never retire,
And ever are watchful and wakeful
And ever are scourging with fire.

But now draweth near the avengers,
The invincible Army of Death—
They charge with the rush of a whirlwind
And scatter the worms with their breath.

And the sound of the wearisome struggle
And the thought of that terrible fight
Pass on as a dream that the devils
Have whispered to us in the night.

DEATH

Amid the winding woods of Love
I made my weary heart a nest,
And I was happy in the dream,
And said, "Love is the best."

And in the bloody Sea of Lust
I wallowed without pause or rest,
I lived but in a wanton's smile,
And said, "Sin is the best."

At last drew nigh the Reaper Death,
Who came to me a welcome guest,
And then I lay me down and slept,
And said, "Death is the best."

TEARS OF MINE

O tears of mine, thou canst not melt her heart!
The golden birds of day may sob their ancient songs
Into her pearly ear—she will not list.
The sombre birds of night may moan their music
And shroud her memories in deathless dreams,
But still she will not hear.

O dewy heights of heaven, how far away!
O endless Hills of Time, how hard to scale!
O dreams, sweet dreams, how like realities!
O tears of mine, thou canst not melt her heart!

VOICELESS

I feel unuttered melodies,
I tread the far world-dotted way,
I strive in vain to touch the keys
That lead the soul toward the skies—
The music deep within me dies
Nor sees the blessed light of day.

My wild heart roams beyond the stars,
But only knows a plaintive wail,
While something still within me bars
The dreams from being more than sighs—
The music deep within me dies
And leaves my grief an untold tale.

AURORA

Far in the shell-tinted halls of morn
She dwelleth all alone.
Bathed in a shroud of myriad tears,
She maketh gentle moan.
Her voice is the sob of a distant sea,
So sad and sweet its tone.

And the burden rings of the song she sings
In the steps of the sun as it flies,
Awaiting a lover that cometh not
Amid the purple skies—
Awaiting a heart that is dead and cold
And heareth not her sighs.

THE MOANING DOVE

The moaning of the mateless dove
Is heard, a mournful wail,
And the passionless eyes of weary Night
Grow sad as they hear the tale.

Grow sad as they hear the sorrowful tale
Of the moaning, mateless dove,
Whilst the wondering moon in pity looks
And the stars weep tears of love.

But its love has flown with another mate
To a land beyond the sea,
And the night winds sob as they pass along
And weep for sympathy.

Ah, me! the hearts that a woman's face
May cause to fade and die
Would reach from the depths of farthest Hell
To the end of the golden sky.

IF I SHOULD KISS THEE

If I should kiss thee, sweet,
Those lips of honey dew,
My heart would melt away
And die for love of you—
If I should kiss thee, sweet.

If I should kiss thee, sweet—
Those maddening eyes of fire—
The barriers of Fate would melt
In the breath of Love's desire—
If I should kiss thee, sweet.

IMMORTALITY

The simple fading of a flower
Has more of pathos than a nation's fall—
The simple fading of a flower,
The greatest tragedy of all.
And this our life is as a flower, too,
With more of grief than e'er a flower knew,
But with'ring and dying e'en as the flowers do.
And thus it goes from dreary day to day;
The things we love are first to fade away.
Fading away to what? Living only to die,
While on our knees to a cold, impassive sky
We ask and pray, and may not know the why.
But still within our heart there lives a hope,
When all is said, the weary strife is o'er,
Beyond the sorrow and the endless pain,
Beyond the darkness where we blindly grope—
The rose we loved shall lift its head again.

DREAMS

Through all the weary night I lie and dream of her,
A shadow worshiped and a shadow worshiper;
And when the peeping dawn comes with her gift of day
I slowly drain the dreams that morning takes away.

My world is built of dreams, and love, and truth,
Sweet fragile dreams, alas! that only come to youth;
And life is but a dream that gods more grand
Have dreamed and given us to understand.

THE ROSE

There once grew a rose in the Vale of the Shade
That fell from the lands above,
As red as a blush on the cheek of a maid,
As sweet as the breath of love.

And this is the song the red rose sung
With a voice so strange and sad
That the birds in the cloudless blue o'erhung
To list, and their hearts were glad:

"I am the Flower of Life so fair
That blooms 'mid the wastes of Night;
I know no sorrow, I have no care,
And my bloom shall ever be bright."

Long it flourished and long it grew,
Kissed by each wind's light breath;
But around and around it, too,
Coiled the noisome weeds of Death.

Around and in, as the mouth of a leech,
And at last they grew so high
That the winds of heaven no more could reach,
Nor the sun of God's bright sky.

And so it faded, and drooped and died,
And sings no more its song;
The angels high in the heavens sighed,
But the King of Death is strong.

The Rose of the Valley blooms no more,
The lilies they weep for love,
And nothing is heard but the deep sea's roar,
And the moan of the mateless dove.

I SAT ALONE

I sat alone in a waste of sand
And watched the pale moon rise—
The radiant light of the deathless stars
Was flooding all the skies.

I heard as in a passing dream
The moan of the sombre sea,
And my heart went out for a love of loves
To share the dream with me.

I fain would have laid my weary heart
To sleep beside the wave,
For all of death seemed a solemn smart
And all of life a grave!

LOVE AND CHANGE

When the flower of youth has faded,
And gone the fire from her eye,
And from her cheeks the roses are fled,
And the sleep of death draws nigh;
When age comes on with its terrors,
Will you call to mind your vow,
And remember the promise you made her,
And love as you love her now?

Ah! 'tis but a fleeting phantom,
This story so sweet and old:
Far better to live a loveless life
Than to see a love grow cold.

Ed. note: The fourth line, in the original edition, ends with the word
"night". I have changed it to "nigh" based on the rhyme and context,
certainly the correct word.

THE PLAYTHING

The heart of a man is a thing of clay
That the hand of a woman takes,
And shapes and fashions, then throws away—
Or perhaps she keeps and breaks.

I FAIN WOULD REST

I fain would rest my weary soul,
And all the world's, it seems,
From striving for a mystic goal
That lives but in our dreams.

And I would lie upon Love's heart
And pillow on Love's breast
Through aeons of unending smart
To lull the soul to rest.

But I shall fight with mortal breath,
Nor perish in the strife,
For sullen are the shades of Death
And bright the ways of Life.

HEART'S DESIRE

When the wild wind sigheth
My dream-soul flies
To a land that lieth
Beyond the skies.

When the bleak night cometh
I wing my way
Through purple heavens
To the halls of day.

My wild heart cries
When the pale moon gleams
For a world of sighs
And a land of dreams.

LOVE

A man's love changeth as the sea
And passeth with the passing sun.
A woman's heart may love but one,
And that for all Eternity.

AND WE FORGET

No love can live beyond the tomb—
The tide of life is rolling on,
And o'er our lives Death casts a gloom
As passing clouds obscure the sun.

A week, a month, a year of vain regret;
A sob, a sigh, a tear and we forget.

And still we dance the dance of joy,
And life to us is as a toy
To finger and to cast away,
A plaything of a summer's day.

A week, a month, a year of vain regret;
A sob, a sigh, a tear and we forget.

A DREAM FACE

Far in the cool, shell-tinted halls of morn,
Bathed in an evanescent shroud of tears,
My love of loves sits, weary and forlorn.

The grief of years is written in her eyes
That look into illimitable night,
Brighter than any star that stabs the skies.

Her voice is as the murmur of the sea,
The lap of waves upon a distant shore,
And all attuned to sweetest melody.

I feel the rapture of a long-dead past
Whene'er her spirit passes through my heart—
Sweet as Love's breath, and far too sweet to last.

She waits for me in pitying, tender grace
Far in the boundless realms of love,
But I shall never know nor gaze upon her face.

O LIFE!

O LIFE! rare instrument of many strings
Played by an Infinite Hand. At times it seems
Sweet harmony wells forth at every touch
And every note is one of joy. And then
This sweet old earth seems sweeter than before.
But this too seldom. For that mighty harp
Emits, alas! more discord than sweet sound
And is too oft attuned to tones like tears.

SAPPHO

Far off the low Leucadian shore,
Buried beneath innumerable seas,
Lies one who sang but sings no more
Her golden melodies.

A solitary star above
Keeps watch with never-tiring eyes
On her who sang of deathless love,
Heart-weary of the rolling skies.

And ever on the rising waves
A song so sadly sweet is heard,
The ghastly dead rise from their graves
And listen to the unseen bird

Out of the heart of the sombre deep,
While on and on the murmur runs—
The listening larks are lulled to sleep
And wheel no more the endless suns.

And then a wistful wail it seems,
It floats along the sandy shore,
A voice from out the Land of Dreams—
A sob, a sigh, and then no more.

Ah, sleep in peace, fond, panting heart,
Where thou so long in rest hath slumbered;
O'er thee hath passed the world's cruel smart,
The sighs of centuries unnumbered.

SAPPHO

They steal adown the sombre centuries,
Cleaving the dust of immemorial years,
The sad, sweet songs of passion and of tears
Of her whose wild, immurmurous melodies
Rang in the air by far Leucadian seas.
She sings no more, but Love still knows her tone,
And Death may pause where Love yet claims her own,
And may not pass the door to which Love holds the keys.

From out the deep sea-caverns where she lies,
Along and up into the endless suns,
Beyond the stars, beyond the purple skies,
A dark and deathless murmur runs,
To find its echo in sad hearts, nor shuns
The dead upon whose pallid lips Love breathes and sighs.

SAPPHO

Her golden melodies we hear no more,
Her trembling passion-heart is forever still,
Hushed to eternal rest by soft Leucadian waves,
Whilst sombre suns stare pitilessly down
And strive to pierce the deep sea-caverns where she lies.
The lonely stars may sigh through immemorial years,
The centuries may weep—she hears them not; for now,
Lulled gently to sleep by the rippling music of innumer-
            able seas,
She dreams sweet dreams of death.

SAPPHO

High on the lone Leucadian cliff
She stands engirdled by the sobbing sea,
A starlit splendor written in her eyes,
And on her brow—Eternity.

One moment stays she, lonely one of song,
Touched by the wan moon's wistful, trembling beams,
Then Love and Death are mingled into one—
She meets the loved one of her dreams.

THE DAUGHTER OF THE SKY

O Daughter of the Sky,
Thine eyes are strange and bright,
Daughter of the Sky,
I fear their stinging light.
Thy voice it cannot sound
In the leaden air of earth—
But a lost soul's cry in the wind,
And a new soul come to birth.

O Daughter of the Sky,
From what realm hast thou fled?
"From the halls of the rise of the blood-red moon
And the land of the moaning dead."
As sweet as the winds of Love
Is the sweetness of thy breath,
As sweet as the winds of Love,
But as cold as the winds of Death.

Daughter of the Sky,
I love thee, love thee true.
Daughter of the Sky,
A suitor come to woo!
"Where goest thou so soon?
Ah, leave me not," I said.
But back she fled to the blood-red moon
And the land of the moaning dead.

CHANGE

When first love enters in the heart
'Tis like a sunshine ray—
Brings light and gladness in its path,
And bids us hope alway.

But when 'tis old it waxeth cold
And settles like a shroud—
Instead of hope it brings despair
Instead of light a cloud.

IF WE BUT KNEW!

How many sighs, how many tears
For loved ones passed away
That we could save if we but knew
Of Life and Death—which false, which true,
And what beyond the grave—
      If we but knew!

How many years of weary woe
That might be spent a better way
If we, the seekers after Truth,
Could know the night from day
And choose between the two—
      If we but knew!

THE CRUSHED ROSE

O pale and silent sufferer, whose fragrance sweet
Imparts a gentle odor to the air around!
I lift thee tenderly from off the ground,
Where hard, unheeding feet have trampled thee to death;
I place thee near my heart,
To treasure thee, dear rose, for years to come—
Thou art fit emblem of my bleeding soul,
Which, rent and torn with love yet unreturned,
Lies silent, sad and still and ne'er complains.

THE DIFFERENCE

I never found the earth so fair
As when she told me of her love,
And, looking down into her eyes,
A radiant light as from above
Shone bright and glorious there—
     I never found the earth so fair.

I never found the earth so drear
As when I knew her false to me,
And, looking down into her eyes,
I saw the devilish, mocking glee
Of her whom once I held so dear—
     I never found the earth so drear.

A DREAM FACE

I saw thee once, 'twas long ago,
　　　Since then an endless night of pain,
But though I search for years, I know
　　　That I shall gaze on thee again.

Somewhere, sometime; till then I wait.
　　　('Tis weary waiting all alone).
I pray to God it come not late,
　　　When age is nigh and youth has flown.

And through my soul thine eyes of love
　　　Sent down a pitying mystic gleam,
Foretelling of the worlds above
　　　(Alas! 'twas only in a dream).

'Twas only in a dream, oh, yes!
　　　Then I awoke, and all was o'er.
Such dreams come only once to bless
　　　A joyless life, and then no more.

But though I search through weary years,
　　　Thy face will come to me again,
And though the path be wet with tears,
　　　I shall not look for thee in vain.

DEATH

"Joy from all the earth has fled,
God of Life and Love is dead"—
Thus the maddened lover said.

Looked up to the cold blue sky,
Looked in vain for a reply
Standing by her lonely grave;
God had taken what he gave.
"Leave me here to mourn alone,
Brain and heart have turned to stone;
Leave me grieving by her side,
Leave me with my lovely bride."
Morning came and found him there
In the chill and wintry air,
Spirit fled from world of woes,
To the land that no grief knows -—

To the land of mystic light,
        To the Garden of the Blest,
To the land of hope and dreams,
        Where the weary are at rest.

THE SUICIDE

He sought for things he could not find,
He hunted through the weary years,
The path was watered by his tears,
And Life was cold, though Death was kind.

He sought for love in a woman's heart,
For truth within a woman's eyes—
He sought for truth where falsehood lies
And looked for love where love is not.

He cried to God, but He was dead;
To her, but she did not reply;
He thought perhaps 'twere best to die,
His dreams forever left unsaid.

THE END

The path is steep and the way is dark,
And the wind it bloweth cold,
No signs are there the road to mark
Which smelleth as graveyard mold;
      And the wanderer dreams of Home.

In bygone days there was a light,
But that light long since has flown,
And none may say if the road be right
Which leads to the Great Unknown;
      And the wanderer dreams of Home.

A traveler comes who treads the way,
Whose brave heart knows no fears,
But the mighty tide of Time flows on
And the path is one of tears;
      And the wanderer dreams of Home.

The traveler falleth and dieth,
And no one heeds his cry
But the wild bird as it flieth
In the heights of the topmost sky;
      And the wanderer dreams no more.

To WALTER DECASSERES

EPIPHANY: August 12, 1881.

INGRESSION: February 4, 1900.

RESOLVED

I would not have him back.
He is wave and flame and crescent moon.
He is the bulging, westward-moving night,
The ivory lap and lave they call the dawn,
And he circles with the eagle round and roundabout
       Mont Blanc.

UPRENDERED

He is the slab of light across my door,
A signet set upon the brow of Time—
The Boy that was uprendered to the Light
And flung beyond the gates of Accident.

UNWITHERED

She sepulchred his soul in soft, lascivious flesh,
She gashed his mind with red and purple images,
She rabbled him with frantic, hot desires—
Then called to him from out the Ebon Gate
And with gesture nympholeptic locked him up between
      her breasts.

WAITING

You are not buried where your body lies,
Where Matter and the Worms hold long carouse;
But there, atop the catafalque of Night,
Where Aldebaran has sheened your soul in silver light,
You listen for the bugles of the Dawn,
The heralds of the promised Rendezvous !

PRE-DESTINED

With eye that cleft the many-colored Lure
And smote with godlike mock upon the face of Circum-
       stance,
He plunged with ecstasy into his Dream,
Where now he lies slabbed up in silence.

HOME

No more the fallacies of flesh,
Nor ever to drink in with sickening nostril
The stench of multiplied vain hopes,
Or be the hanger-on to Change,
Or play the bawd to concupiscent sense—
No more, and still no more forever! of these ancient,
      sweet seductions
For him who by a single, swift, inexorable act now reigns
      in Nullibiety.

IMMUNE

He stands a carven image in my brain, the great
      Hellenic frenzy in his eye,
And Time that sucks into her maw the Thee and Me and
      things not yet compounded
Shall touch him not! Shall touch him not!

B. DeC.

www.ingramcontent.com/pod-product-compliance
Lightning Source LLC
Chambersburg PA
CBHW021224020426
42331CB00003B/453